An Unhinged History Book

STICKS 'N' STONES 'N' DINOSAUR BONES

Written by Ted Enik
Illustrated by G.F. Newland

Being a Whimsical "Take" on a (pre)Historical Event

Schiffer Publishing Ltd

4880 Lower Valley Road • Atglen, PA 19310

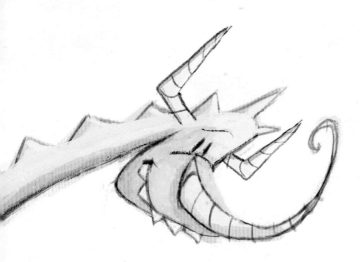

Other Schiffer Books on Related Subjects:

Mesozoic Fossils: Triassic and Jurassic, Bruce L. Stinchcomb, 978-0-7643-3163-3

Mesozoic Fossils II: The Cretaceous Period, Bruce L. Stinchcomb, 978-0-7643-3259-3

Text copyright © 2017 by Ted Enik
Illustrations copyright © 2017 by G.F. Newland

Library of Congress Control Number: 2017935428

Type set in Dude/Gorey

ISBN: 978-0-7643-5394-9
Printed in China

Co-published by Pixel Mouse House &
Schiffer Publishing, Ltd.
4880 Lower Valley Road
Atglen, PA 19310
Phone: (610) 593-1777; Fax: (610) 593-2002
E-mail: Info@schifferbooks.com
Web: www.schifferbooks.com

For our complete selection of fine books on this and related subjects, please visit our website at www.schifferbooks.com. You may also write for a free catalog.

Schiffer Publishing's titles are available at special discounts for bulk purchases for sales promotions or premiums. Special editions, including personalized covers, corporate imprints, and excerpts, can be created in large quantities for special needs. For more information, contact the publisher.

We are always looking for people to write books on new and related subjects. If you have an idea for a book, please contact us at proposals@schifferbooks.com.

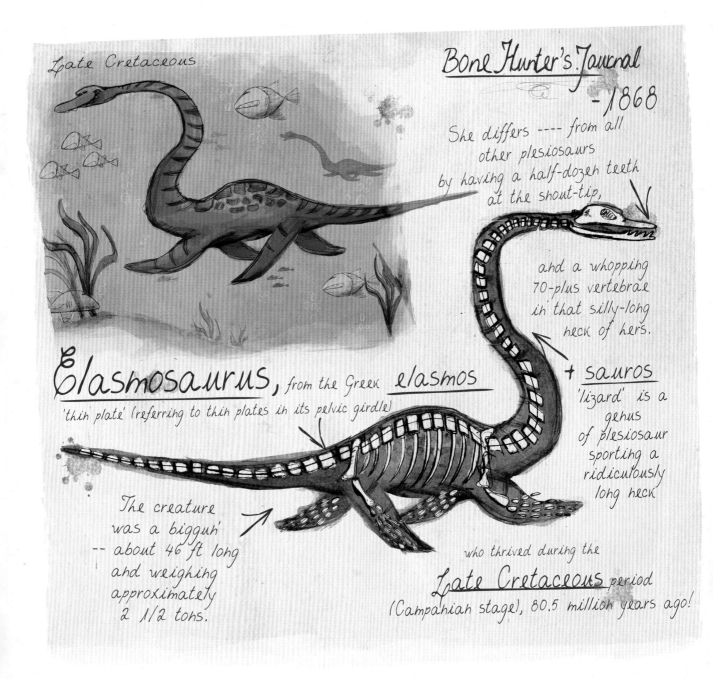

Late Cretaceous

She differs ---- from all
other plesiosaurs
by having a half-dozen teeth
at the snout-tip,

and a whopping
70-plus vertebrae
in that silly-long
neck of hers.

Elasmosaurus, from the Greek _elasmos_
'thin plate' (referring to thin plates in its pelvic girdle)

+ _sauros_
'lizard' is a
genus
of plesiosaur
sporting a
ridiculously
long neck

The creature
was a bigguh'
-- about 46 ft long
and weighing
approximately
2 1/2 tons.

who thrived during the
Late Cretaceous period
(Campanian stage), 80.5 million years ago!

Dedications

For KR (expert eye and Commonlo' Bro'), JRP and JH (unparalleled and patient chums), SR (tireless booster and Muse-in-Law), RPG (mentor and Guiding Star), and LGE (Stardust Sister and early companion in Plastic DinoLand).

With special italicized and underlined thanks to RH for his confidence and encouragement, and for reinventing the World-as-We-Know-It, and to GFN for his (insert mega-superlative) Invention 'n' Creativity, (insert mega-superlative) Endurance, and Friendship -- and for going way-y-y-y "On Beyond Zebra!" in bringing S'n'S to life.

-Ted Enik

For my parents and grands who read to me when I was little, and to my sons, who let me read to them. Special thanks to RH and TE for giving me lots of fun stuff to do, and to the charming Miss S. for encouraging me to do it.

-G.F. Newland

STICKS 'N' STONES 'N' DINOSAUR BONES

BEING A WHIMSICAL "TAKE" ON A (PRE)HISTORICAL EVENT

"THE BONE WARS" refers to a gold rush-like scramble to find the most and "best" dinosaur fossils which took place during America's Gilded Age (between 1865 and the 1890s).

This frenzy of discovery sparked a vicious competition between EDWARD DRINKER COPE (Academy of Natural Sciences in Philadelphia) and O. CHARLES MARSH (Peabody Museum of Natural History at Yale).

Each paleontologist used less-than-ethical methods to outdo the other -- lying, stealing, blackmail, even destroying fossils. Both obsessed and vengeful men attacked each other in professional journals as well as in newspapers targeted at the general public, in an all-out attempt to ruin his rival's credibility and have his funding withdrawn.

INTRODUCING

O. CHARLES MARSH

EDWARD D. COPE

THE BONE HUNTERS

I'll tell you a story -- and some of it's true --
that explores and explains what the Bone Hunters do.

Well, two of them anyway.
Both pioneers,
of a science that studies things
buried for years --

for years upon years
upon years upon years,

upon years upon years,

upon ZILLIONS of years.

The drama begins
pre-the automobile:
when the horse was a car,
and the hoof was the wheel.

Before TVs, and PCs, and FOFLing,
when calling long distance meant
really -- you're YELLING.

When most every gentleman sported a beard,
and ladies wore ringlets, and children appeared
to be little adults -- standing stiller than statues,
allergic to burping, and giggles, and *ah-CHOOs!*

To pin down a date, let's say eighteen and seventy

(one, eight,

five, seven --

plus two,

plus eleven).

Happy Trails to You!

Wrinkled professors from northeastern colleges
saw there was room to expand certain knowledges.

Neighboring farmers and brave mountaineers
had been bringing them oversized fossils for years.

And little-by-little they came to suspect
that these petrified bones would be good to collect

and to carefully study, then put on display!
Greedily guessing what people might pay
to come gawk at these skeleton-monsters of yore.

"Feast your eyes
-- Ladies, Gents -- at

THE GREAT DINOSAUR!"

TICKETS

$$$

So these wrinkled professors -- in two separate groups,
from two universities -- gathered their troops

of well-qualified scholars, the best of the best,
and picked one fellow each to accomplish their quest

to go digging up prizes, surprising! terrific!
(. . . they felt that they needn't be much more specific).

EDWARD D. COPE was the man that School "A"
felt was perfectly suited for digging away!

O. CHARLES MARSH represented School "B."
Who could think of no Bone Hunter better than he!

EDWARD D. COPE
versus
O. CHARLES MARSH

"Instant Enemies" wouldn't describe it too harshly.

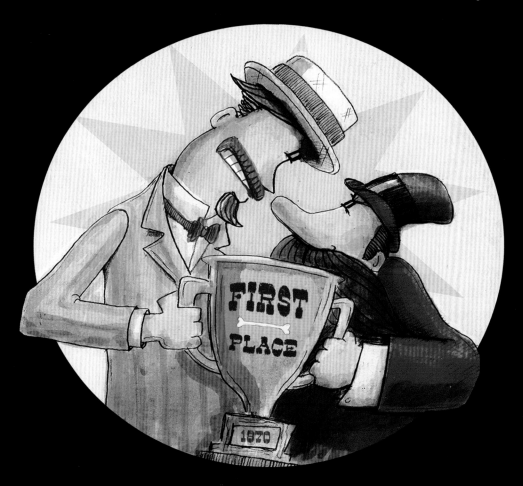

For both were aware what was *really* their mission:
secure for their college the top dog position.

To earn for it honor and bring to it fame,
and the right to be first in the world to proclaim

they put paleontology smack on the map.
Quite a feather for their university's cap!

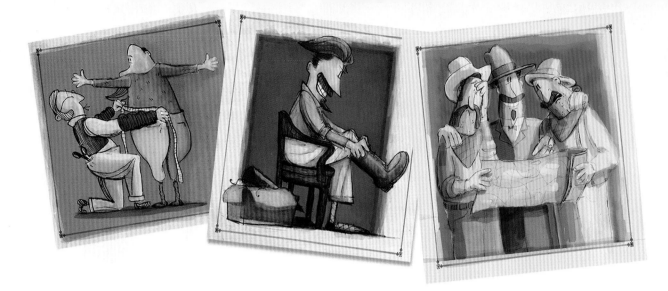

Marsh and Cope got to work -- not a moment to lose! --
buying Bone-Hunter trousers and Bone-Hunter shoes.
And a Bone-Hunter hat with their name stenciled on it,
a handsome and practical sun-screening bonnet.

Both scientists hired (devoted and true)
a professional scavenger hunter, or two,
and a master of hounds, and a cook, and a guide,
and a camel -- because they're amusing to ride.

Between them they packed more than eight hundred crates,
then shipped them by rail to the great western states,
where the valleys are deep and the deserts are wide,
because that's where the fossils apparently hide.

Cope chose Colorado 'cause everyone knows
that there's wonders aplenty on top of plateaus.
And Marsh took Nebraska 'cause once he was there he
could putter for treasure across the vast prairie.

They weathered the journey with nary a hitch
and got down to work at a *feverish* pitch.

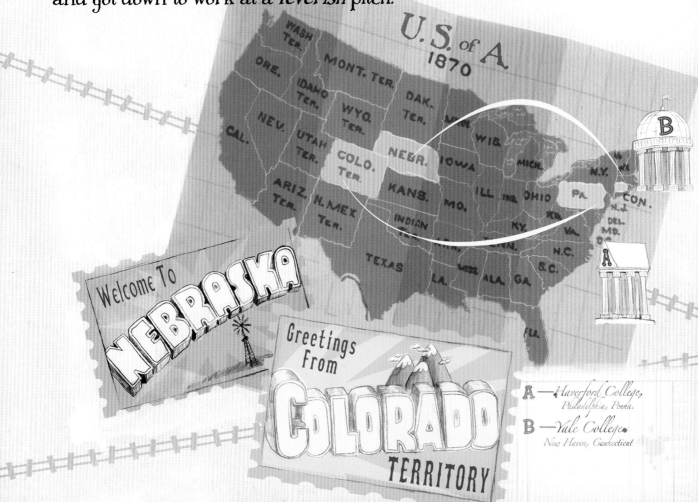

A —Haverford College,
Philadelphia, Penna.
B —Yale College,
New Haven, Connecticut

They busted the boulders, they sifted the slabs
and the riverbeds swarming with petrified crabs.

Cope fancied the pick-ax, the chisel, the awl,
while Marsh used his tweezers -- he wasn't as tall.

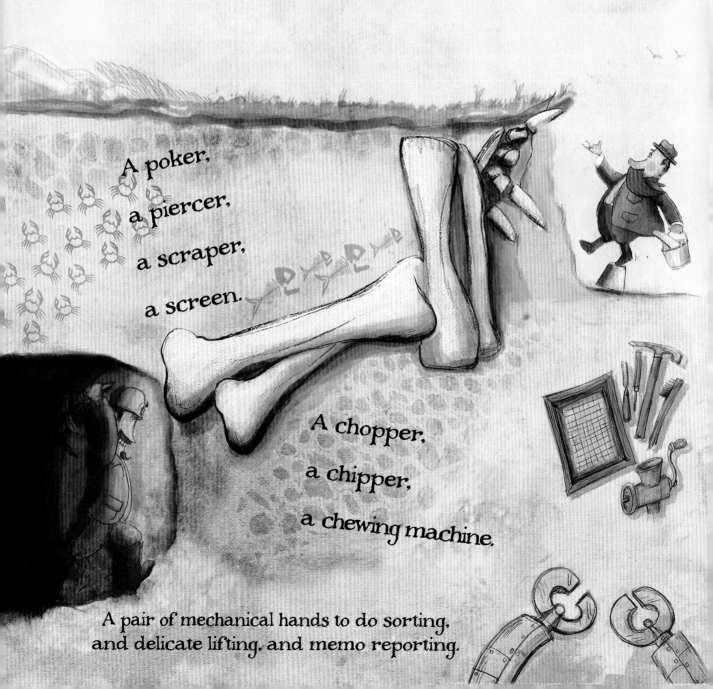

A poker,

a piercer,

a scraper,

a screen.

A chopper,

a chipper,

a chewing machine.

A pair of mechanical hands to do sorting,
and delicate lifting, and memo reporting.

Before very long, nearly quick as a cough,
these Bone Hunters' efforts began to pay off!

"Well, son-of-a-gun!" boasted Marsh to his men,
"This dinosaur egg would impress any hen!"

"Well, don't that beat everything!" Dr. Cope crowed,
"A big pair of piggy-toe bones in the road!"

As their digging went on and they found more and more,
they also found out they were both keeping score.

Dot · Dot · Dash!

Each daily discovery --

certain to stun --

went leapfrogging over

the previous one.

If any bone promised a glimmer of glory,
a scout set about telegraphing the story
to big city newspapers -- holding their deadlines --
and poised to report it in EXTRA LARGE headlines.

And little by little,

one bone at a time,

"Discovery" slowly

gave over to . . .

"CRIME!"

The Glo
"I SAW A DINOSAUR"
said Marsh

The Inquirer
News of the Day   3rd December 1874
TRICERATOPS
COPE FINDS
65,000,000
YEAR OLD
FOSSIL!

Story continues on pages 3-8

"To heck with the science," Marsh hissed to his shovel.
"Outshining my rival's the goal, far above all."

"It's much more important to outdo my foe,
and if fibbing comes into it, who's going to know?"

Awake in his sleeping bag, miles away,
Cope swore in a similar manner to stray

off the path straight and narrow, and do all it took
to belittle his colleague by hook or by CROOK!

And so, then and there, unbeknownst to each other,
both gents made a pledge to one-better his brother:

to fully commit to a scallywag's scheme
in hopes to become THE *Bone Hunter Supreme!*

To put it another way, play the reporter,
and cut to the chase, make a long story shorter;
when "real" discoveries weren't enough,
the gentlemen started unearthing *pure fluff*.

If Marsh hit the news with a "Watchumacaurus,"
then Cope answered back with his "Thingamasaurus."
When Cope, after breakfast, unveiled an "Inventon,"
a tick before dinner, Marsh found a "Pretendon."

"Incredible-docus," a "NeverWas Rex,"
a "LetsSeeHowLongICanFoolYou-ter-x."
A "Fake-us," a "Fraud-us," a "Phonybalone-us,"
a "LookOverThereAndPleaseLeaveMeAlone-us."

Their ruthless one-upmanship
grew so fanatic
that one of them *had* to do
something dramatic --

A MAJOR
ANNOUNCEMENT,

a moment enthralling,

AN ENDING,

a
FINISH,

a "Once and for All-ing!"

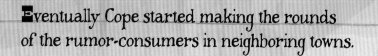

Eventually Cope started making the rounds
of the rumor-consumers in neighboring towns.

Dropping hints here and there, sort of lighting the fuse,
that he's sitting on earth- (and bone-) shattering NEWS!

That he'd found something *special*, a precious-rare wonder,
a skeleton sure to blow others asunder.

So he plasters up posters
"COME ONE AND COME ALL!
to the
LADIES-AND-GENTS
WHO-LIKE-LISTENING
HALL!"

In the center of town,
at the end of the week,

"WHERE IT'S
GUARANTEED
YOU'LL BE SHOWN
SOMETHING
UNIQUE!"

PROFESSOR COPE'S
?
PRECIOUS
RARE WONDER
COME ONE, COME ALL AND SEE THE
NEW DINOSAUR SKELETON
at
THE LADIES & GENTS WHO LIKE LISTENING HALL
Admission - 10 Cents
DON'T MISS IT!!

On the night of the gathering everyone stood
in a circle on scaffolding made out of wood,

covered-over with canvas and painted with creatures
that sported a sortment of *dinosaur* features.

The crowd had surrounded -- and stared at dumbstruck,
a "mystery" roughly the size of a duck,

fully hidden beneath a red calico cloth.
Growing antsy they started-in nervously coughing.

Cope made his grand entrance, bowed silent and lowly,
consulted his notes, then began his speech slowly.

"Dear fans of the fossil, so glad you could come.
You're about to be shown quite a 'dinger de hum.'

"Petrified bits of a giant, a titan --
whose belly, I'm sure, you could all spend the night in.

"The beast was *so long*, when it ventured to roam
its nose met its tail as it circled back home.

"The beast was *so tall* . . . when it wanted a swim,
the ocean expanded to make room for him.

"Ten Matterhorns high and ten Grand Canyons wide,
with squiggles and dots decorating its side."

(A Magic Lantern Projector!)

"Its forest of tentacles, feelers, and spines,
would mimic an army of squid-porcupines.

"Its meadow of body-hair, feathers, and scales,
would bring to mind bunches of parakeet-whales."

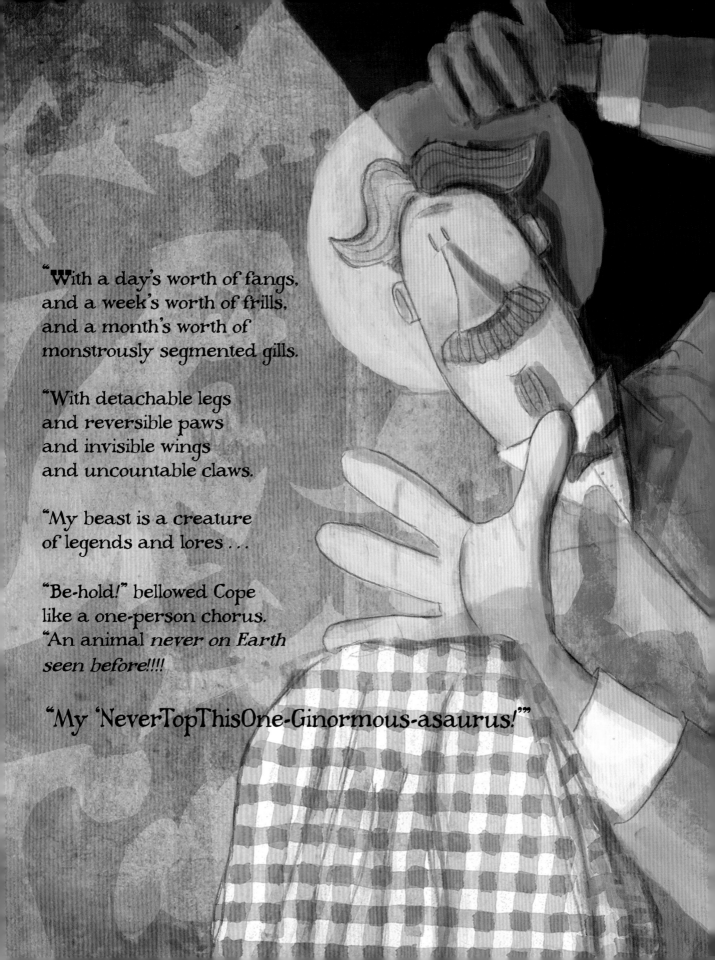

"With a day's worth of fangs,
and a week's worth of frills,
and a month's worth of
monstrously segmented gills.

"With detachable legs
and reversible paws
and invisible wings
and uncountable claws.

"My beast is a creature
of legends and lores . . .

"Be-hold!" bellowed Cope
like a one-person chorus.
"An animal *never on Earth
seen before!!!!*

"My 'NeverTopThisOne-Ginormous-asaurus!'"

With a flick of his wrist
the man tugged off the covering,
causing the crowd to redouble its hovering
over what looked like a skeleton cat --

with a little bit "fish" and a little bit "bat"
fastened-on, thereabouts, in *unusual* places.
The people, they put on their skeptical faces.

"It's a *baby* Ginormous-asaurus you see."
Added Cope in a panic, "Its parents were easily
twenty times larger -- NO! Thirty, I'm guessing."
But soon he could see that he wasn't impressing
his audience much. And a few of them winced.
Even fewer went home absolutely convinced.

Well!
It took several weeks for the buzz to subside.
And it took even longer for Marsh to decide

how to manage his counterpunch, stage a reprisal
so stunning, so crushing that everyones' eyes'll

pop out of their heads and start rolling around,
like a party of hard boiled eggs on the ground.

First he rented a tent for one night (with a band!)
of imported performers from North Ireland.

Then he bought some balloons, and a crop of confetti,
and crepe paper streamers that looked like spaghetti.

With everything ready, Marsh rigged a big banner
across the Town Square where he knew every manner

of person would see it, then plan to attend
the event where Cope's fortune would come to an end.

EXTRAVAGA-SAURUS!
• REVEALED •

On the evening in question, the big top was filled
with a jumble of people undoubtedly thrilled
to be there for the making of dinosaur news.
So preparing with care, Marsh decided to choose . . .

. . . the precisest-right moment -- the height of excitement,
a fizzing of frenzy, the peak of delightment.
He took center ring, working hard to look splendid,
his hand in the air with its pinky extended.

Exclaiming, "Good People, look here! Feast your eyes!
What I'm holding before you -- though tiny in size --
is by far-and-away, of the hundreds I've found,
quite the topmost dead treasure I took from the ground!"

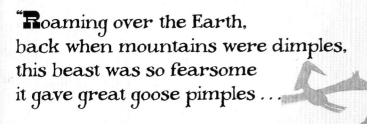

"**R**oaming over the Earth,
back when mountains were dimples,
this beast was so fearsome
it gave great goose pimples . . .

". . . to any-and-everything --
crawling or flying,
or scaly or furry,
or living or dying."

"LISTEN!"

"Evidence shows,
and it's quite the surprise,
that the beastie had hundreds of
button-size eyes."

"ALSO,

"Clues have been found --
causing hooting and cheers --
that the beast had a million
reptilian-type ears."

"Its deafening roaring
turned glaciers to slush,
and vast deserts to pudding,
and moorlands to mush.

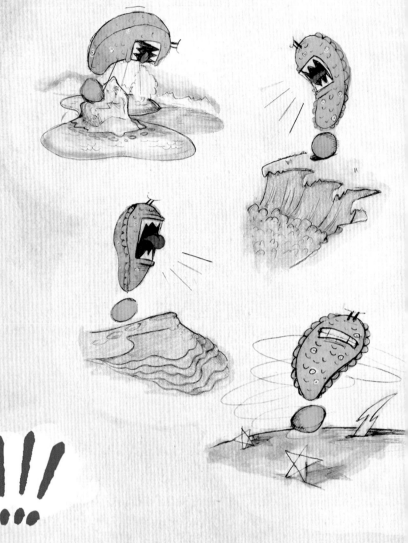

"Its sinister hissing
unbended bolt-lightning,
unraveled tornadoes,
and stopped stars from bright'ning."

"**W**ith legs like an ostrich, and arms like an ape,
and a lasso-like tail nothing much could escape.

"With red-leather wings the thing struck you as being
The Devil himself . . . only smaller, you see.

"And you've noticed, I'm certain, how super-colossal is
this very *rarest and finest of fossils!!!!*

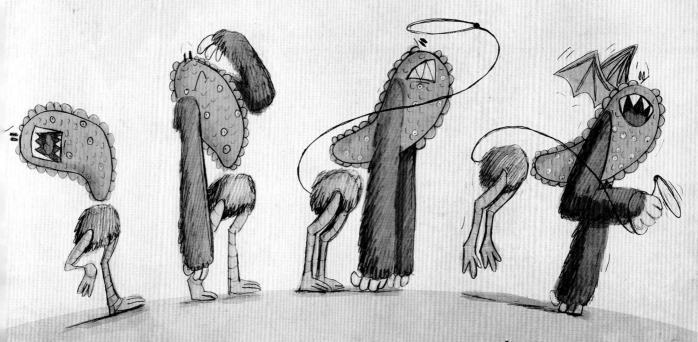

"It clearly surpasses all comers before; it's my
'WhoAreYouKidding?-Extravaga-saurus!'"

WELL...

The crowd scratched their heads altogether as one,
and then squinted as though they looked into the sun.

Until Marsh applied pressure: "A mountain of stones
needed blasting to get at this Crown Prince of Bones.

"And ... and, honest-and-truly, no other explorer
than I could have brought you this fine dinosaur."

THEN...

The whispers began like a swarming of bees:
"I can't quite .... I don't .... Point it out to me, PLEASE."

"Now, you didn't, perhaps, leave it home?" teased the Mayor.
Which got Marsh's face to grow anxious and grayer.

He puffed himself up and he started to bluster
so brashly it tapped all the strength he could muster.

"What's wrong with you peasants, you rubes!? Can it be
you're all dumb as an ox and unable to see ...

"It's THE most historic fantastical find,
balanced HERE on my left little finger? You blind?!"

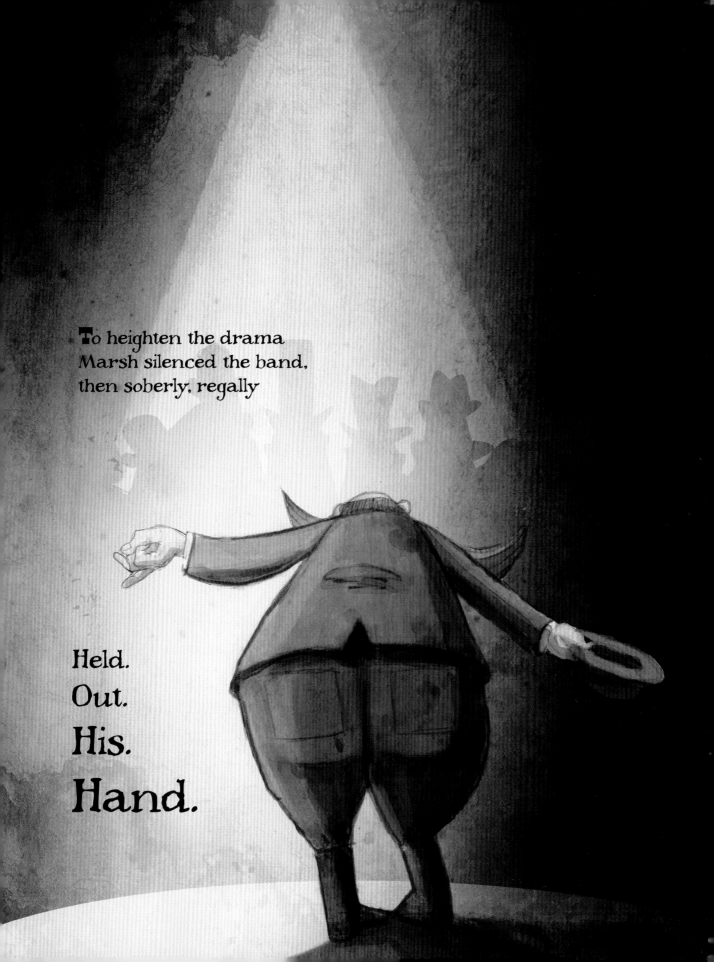

To heighten the drama
Marsh silenced the band,
then soberly, regally

Held.
Out.
His.
Hand.

Folks took a step forward, then took a step back,
then took a short break 'cause they wanted a snack.

Ah, but soon Marsh's audience started to mumble,
to cuss and complain, and guffaw, and to hum.

For they couldn't quite praise what they couldn't quite see,
prompting Marsh to remark,

"Well then don't look at me!!!"

So they didn't, and wouldn't do ever again.
The whole world turned its back on both dinosaur men.

Like *that!* The Bone Hunters were fired, and broke.
Where once they were famous they now were a joke.

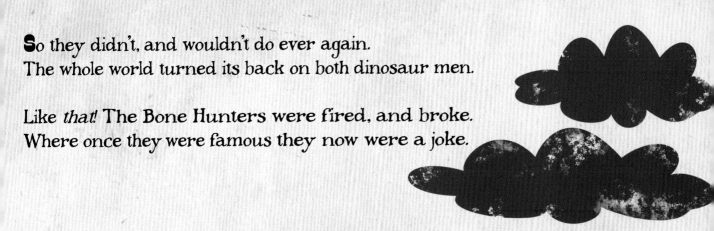

And why not? They *were* phonies
and Bone Buccaneers

who swindled their sponsors
and spoiled their careers.

But . . . ignoring the lying, the cheating, the stealing,
and setting aside the insane double-dealing,

despite *some* discoveries being untrue-ish,
the duo deserves a fair chapter or two.

Even though their behavior was childish, sophomoric,
they added aplenty to work prehistoric --

before they went crazy and everything soured.
Because of them paleontology *flowered.*

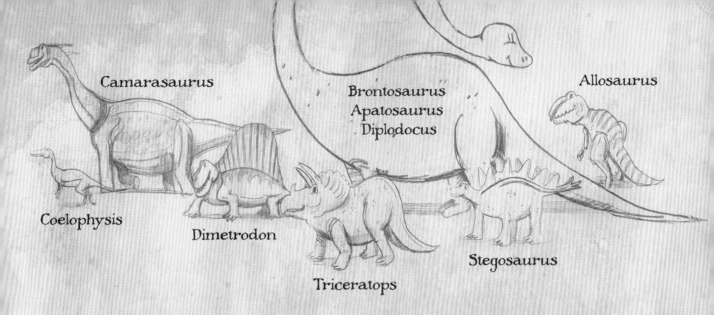

Camarasaurus

Brontosaurus
Apatosaurus
Diplodocus

Allosaurus

Coelophysis

Dimetrodon

Triceratops

Stegosaurus

Their early "Eurekas!" are very well-known,
and lots of their fossils are still being shown:

This-a-saurs, That-a-saurs, Dinos and Deenos,
and hundreds of others that fall in-betweenos.

Elasmosaurus -- Marsh was right!
The head belongs where *he* is pointing!

If you don't believe me, I swear you can see 'em
In any town's Natural History Museum!

The End

<u>ALLOSAURUS</u> ("Different Lizard" in Greek)
Pronounced al-oh-SORE-us.
Discovered and named by Marsh in 1877.
Lived on the plains of North America during the
 Late Jurassic Period, about 155-150 million years ago.

<u>APATOSAURUS</u> originally misnamed "Brontosaurus"
 ("Deceptive Lizard" in Greek)
Pronounced a-PAT-oh-SORE-us.
Discovered and named by Marsh in 1877.
Lived in the forests of North America during the
 Late Jurassic Period, about 154-150 million years ago.
Marsh wrongly thought that adult Apatosaurus bones
 were those of an entirely new dinosaur and named
 it Brontosaurus. It took till 1972 for paleontologists to
 discover his mistake.

<u>DIPLODOCUS</u> ("Double Beam" in Greek)
Pronounced dip-LOW-doe-kuss.
Discovered by Benjamin Mudge and
 Samuel W. Williston in 1877.
Named by Marsh 1878.
Lived on the plains of
 North America during the
 Late Jurassic Period, about
 155-145 million years ago.

<u>STEGOSAURUS</u> ("Roofed Lizard" in Greek)
Pronounced STEG-oh-SORE-us.
Discovered by M. P. Felch in 1876.
Named by Marsh in 1877.
Lived in the forests of North America
 during the Late Jurassic Period,
 about 155-150 million years ago.

<u>TRICERATOPS</u> ("Three-Horned Face" in Greek)
Pronounced try-SEH-rah-tops.
Discovered by John Bell Hatcher in 1887.
Named by Marsh in 1888.
Lived in the forests of North America
 during the Late Cretaceous Period,
 about 68-65 million years ago.

CAMARASAURUS ("Chambered Lizard" in Greek)
Pronounced cam-AH-rah-SORE-us.
Discovered by Oramel W. Lucas in 1877.
Named by Cope in 1877.
Lived on the plains of North America during the
    Late Jurassic Period, about 155-145 million years ago.

COELOPHYSIS ("Hollow Form" in Greek)
Pronounced SEE-low-FIE-sis.
Discovered by David Baldwin in 1881.
Named by Cope in 1889.
Lived on the western plains of North America during
    the Late Triassic Period, about 220 million years ago.

DIMETRODON ("Two Measures of Teeth" in Greek)
Pronounced die-MET-roe-don.
Discovered by unknown
Named by Cope in 1878.
Lived in the swamplands of North America
  during the Permian Period, about 275 million years ago.
Dimetrodon, in fact, was not a dinosaur, but a type of
  reptile called a Synapsid (sih-NAP-sid), of the
  Pelycosaur (PEL-i-kuh-sawr) variety.

Named by
EDWARD D. COPE

ELASMOSAURUS ("Ribbon Lizard" in Greek)
Pronounced el-LAZZ-moe-SORE-us.

Discovered by Dr. Theophilus Turner in 1868. Named by Cope in 1868. Lived in the seas of North America during the Late Cretaceous Period, about 80 million years ago.

Cope and Marsh's feud really began when Marsh noted that his colleague had wrongly placed the skull of an Elasmosaurus at the end of its long tail, rather than onto its similarly long neck (an understandable goof). Marsh's scholarly "nyah-nyah" exploded into decades of ferocious one-upmanship during which both men used their considerable fortunes to tear-up America's deserts looking for more and more dinosaur bones they could name and claim for themselves.

Taking the long view, science itself was the real beneficiary of Cope and Marsh's serious-silly rivalry, as the drive to one-better each other resulted in years of feverish discovery.

Tallying-up their finds, it was Marsh who actually won the "Bone Wars." Here's the final score: Marsh 80 / Cope 56. Combined, they claimed to have discovered more than 142 new species of dinosaurs. Today's paleontologists accept only . . . 32.

photo by JR Pepper / www.girlduality.com

TED ENIK, author, has worked as an illustrator for most of the well-known publishing houses in New York, applying his versatility to both original art as well as classic and current chidren's book characters. Once part of the favored stable of Magic School Bus artists, tapped to fill Hilary Knight's venerable shoes by illustrating the latest Eloise hardcover, *Eloise in Hollwood*, he is currently the artist for the popular Fancy Nancy I Can Read™ series and beavering-away on a bunch of Seuss-inspired Unhinged History and science books.

Visit his website: tedenik.com

G.F. NEWLAND, illustrator, has held a long and ponderous chain of odd jobs over the years, and some were quite horrible indeed. So to pass the time, he doodled. Many of these doodles have made their way into books and frames and onto buttons, bags, posters, and T-shirts, etc.; published by the likes of Scholastic and Hachette, Pixel Mouse House, and Schiffer Publishing, too; and into galleries and museums around the known world (i.e., Brooklyn). His favorite odd jobs to date include being a dad; working at School of Visual Arts, in NYC, where he got his masters in animation; and playing guitar, etc., in a power pop band called The Thigh Highs.

Visit his website: gfnewland.com

. . . WHO SAID WHAT!? . . .

unhingedhistory.com
pixelmousehouse.com